Henrietta Lily

Rosen
REAL
READERS

Rosen
Classroom™
New York

1

The earth is full of air.

Air is made of gas.

People and animals
need air to live.

Air is all around us.

We breathe air.

We breathe through
our mouth and nose.
We get oxygen from the air.
We need oxygen to live.

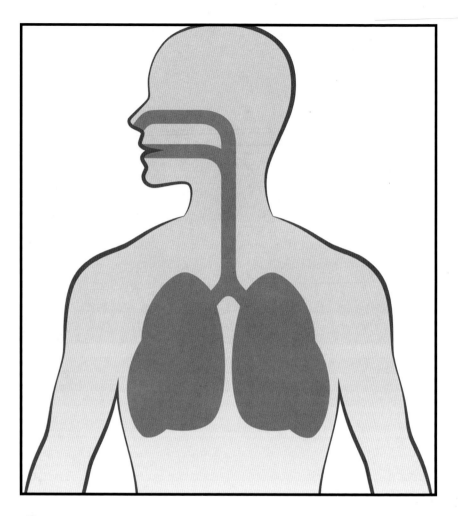

Oxygen moves
through our lungs.

We breathe out carbon dioxide.
Carbon dioxide goes
into the air.

Plants take in carbon dioxide.

This cleans the air.

It is healthy to breathe clean air.

Dirty air is unhealthy to breathe.
It makes us sick.

People need oxygen
wherever they go.
This astronaut has
an oxygen tank.
It lets him breathe in space.

This diver has
an oxygen tank.
It lets her breathe underwater.

Words to Know

astronaut

diver

earth

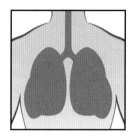

lungs

oxygen tank

plants